NIGHT WATCHES

Inventions on the Life of Maria Mitchell

Also by Carole Oles

The Loneliness Factor
Quarry

NIGHT WATCHES

Inventions on the Life of Maria Mitchell

Carole Oles

ALICE JAMES BOOKS

Cambridge, Massachusetts

I want to thank for their assistance on Nantucket Dr. Emilia P. Belserene, Director of the Maria Mitchell Observatory; Dr. Louise Hussey, Librarian at the Peter Foulger Library; Dr. Jane Stroup, Director of the Maria Mitchell Science Library; Barbara Andrews, Librarian at the Atheneum; and Dr. Wesley N. Tiffney, Director of the University of Massachusetts Biological Field Station.

Special thanks to Max, Hilda, and Martha for their advice and encouragement, and to Steve.

Copyright © 1985 by Carole Oles

Second Printing

Book and Cover Design by Susan Graham
Composition by Ruth Goodman
This book is typeset in Palatino.

Printed in the United States of America.

The publication of this book was made possible with support from the National Endowment for the Arts, Washington, DC, and from the Massachusetts Council on the Arts and Humanities, a state Agency whose funds are recommended by the Governor and appropriated by the State Legislature.

Library of Congress Catalogue Card Number 85.70621
ISBN: Cloth   0–914086–56–1
        Paper   0–914086–57–X

Alice James Books are published by the Alice James Poetry Cooperative, Inc.

Alice James Books
138 Mt. Auburn Street
Cambridge, Massachusetts 02138

Cover photograph taken by Margaret Harwood at the Maria Mitchell Observatory, 1957.

Frontispiece photograph taken by Vail Bros., Poughkeepsie: Maria Mitchell with her student and successor at Vassar, Mary Whitney.

CONTENTS

III

FOREWORD

I could say my intention in this book is to bring Maria Mitchell back alive to a contemporary audience. Though I would be pleased if that were the effect of these poems, it is not why I wrote them. I was drawn to Maria Mitchell by private imperatives seeking satisfactions all their own.

To know Maria I used her journals and diaries, articles by and about her, and the two biographies *Maria Mitchell: Life, Letters, and Journals,* Compiled by Phebe Mitchell Kendall (Boston: Lee and Shepard, 1896) and *Sweeper in the Sky* by Helen Wright (New York: Macmillan Publishing Co., 1949).

While writing I felt inhabited by Maria's personality and ideas. In some of these poems her words or their essence are interwoven with mine. Other poems are total inventions— extrapolated from fact, and true I hope with that truth imagination can tell.

THE CHARLESTOWN ENTERPRISE
EXCLUSIVE ON MARIA, 1884

She was the woman predestined by Providence to show
the world that the American female mind is capable
of digesting mathematics in its entirety. It is true
some of them make crazy-quilts which is against the sex
intellectually, but one Maria Mitchell counts for more
than a million of these. She is our most distinguished living
astronomer of either sex. *She was predestined to show.*

Her hair is white but her black eyes sparkle with all
the fire of youth. Intellectual people never grow old.
To the best of one's knowledge, she has never in a single
instance refused to tell her age, which is the severest
possible test of intellectual strength in a woman.

The girl inherited her father's passion for mathematics.
She has his mind and brain over again.
Very early, when most girls are still in the candy-eating
and tear-shedding age, she became her father's assistant.
The one fact which brought her into fame was her discovery
of the great comet of 1847. She made a mathematical
calculation of its course and the paper is now in
the Smithsonian Institute. *She was the woman predestined.*

The girl astronomer lived a single life. In a confidential
moment one day she confessed that it was much harder
for girls to keep from being married than to marry,
which is undoubtedly true. It requires far more heroism.

She has been working regularly on a salary 48 years,
without a break. Few persons, man or woman can
say as much. She began as Nantucket town librarian.
So small things lead to large. *She is our most distinguished,
she was predestined, one Maria Mitchell counts for more.*
The past 19 years she has been Professor at Vassar College.
Her heart is in her science and with her Vassar girls.
She says they have given her a nobler view of mankind.

I

"I have had a fit of despondency in consequence of being obliged to renounce my own observations as too rough for use. The best that can be said of my life so far is that it has been industrious, and the best that can be said of me is that I have not pretended to be what I was not."

DIARY ENTRY, 1854

MARIA'S GHOST CONSIDERS
INTERPRETATION BY FREUD

So Father was mine.
We all needed male teachers.
He counted on me as I counted for him
how many seconds made an eclipse.
That year I turned twelve.
He taught me to calculate orbits, positions,
to sweep the skies we shared—
Sally, Ann, William, Francis, Andrew, Phebe, Henry, Kate
stayed below—just Father and I
climbing from attic to walkway
to sit at the crown of the house.
Moon rippled the leaftops,
cascaded down Father's back.
His sleeve brushed my hand as I wrote.
Other girls walked the roofs
three years and more looking for Fathers
who would bring whale oil and tea.
But he was here close
in our nightwork while the clock of seasons chimed
and Mother lay under quilts near his portrait
and the rat in our cold cellar gnawed through a sack.
Our eyes studied the heavens together.
The notebooks are locked in a cabinet
that tries to keep out the sea.
I heard someone say you can't tell
where his hand stops and mine begins.

OBSERVING HALLEY'S COMET, 1835

Tonight we know we must look up.
You tamed the errant bodies
by predicting this one,
tracing it to 240 B.C.

Another art: not to see what is not.

The ancients believed comets
brought famine, plague, and war.
Historian Josephus blamed
your comet for Jerusalem's fall.
Observers claimed that it
foretold the Battle of Hastings
and the death of Hal.

Now faint, faint, scarcely
in the transit, the glowing
horsetail streams across the sky . . .
Father and I may be the first
to see it on these shores . . .

What prophecy tonight? The comet
cries *Design* to comfort us
though this sighting be
our one life's time.
What shall I fear? I am 17

and pray to use my open eyes.

MARIA'S GHOST CONSIDERS THE REAPPEARANCE
OF HALLEY'S COMET IN 1985

So far
beyond the farthest nil
inside my coma
I want my voice back
I want to orbit in

and point the IRAS
toward new comets
almost too many
for our alphabet to name

and read your cameras
with electric sensors tracking, testing
Dr. Whipple's dirty snowball model

Already two long lifetimes
since we marked this comet
swing above our upturned isle
Then I felt no augury

In 1985 I fear
not what the comet brings not
heated gas or dust
but what humanity would bring itself

a winter more cold than faded stars
the planet without green
no eyes to search the dark

This same animal leaves footprints on the moon!

You, there—
keep watch

I see, I only
see

"MISS MITCHELL'S COMET"

October 1, 1847, 10:30. Finally the cover
has lifted. That cannot be mist
at 5 degrees above Polaris, where late
as Tuesday nothing was. Does sight
betray? Stay calm. If it be sent
to test, take the test then. No

nebula could have held that place unnoticed
all year. I swept over and over
the quadrant. Was I a sentry
whose watching grew remiss,
the nebula slipping past my sight?
Take notes, hand. After, let head postulate

this seeming comet, new word on the slate
of sky. *October 2.* The object has no
train, appears more brilliant, sighted
now tracking toward the Pole, a rover
we cannot dismiss.
Father says news should be sent

to William Bond at Harvard. I dissent.
What if our find comes late,
the comet an old one we have always missed?
I dread error. But not to know
is the germ that breeds discovery.
The seer must avow the sight.

October 5. Hurtling still, in sight
when it occults a star, the comet's center
within a second of the star which overwhelms
its brightness. I calculate
the point where two celestial nobles
meet, where nothing seems mistake.

Once a man's voice pierced the dark—"Miss,
what are you doing there?"—shook my sight.
Spiders, ticks, even rats had visited, but no
person until he made his arboreal ascent
to find out what lone women do so late
on rooftops, with only sky for cover.

Mister, with nature's consent I climb to sight,
to know the heavens. Later I must sleep. Here
are comets to discover.

DR. ASA GRAY EATS CROW

You think plants aren't hard to know?
I studied them before she was born
to that extraordinary man.
Of course he trained her. Chance
made her look when the comet passed
above Nantucket, tracking West.
So she got to be first of her sex
admitted to the Academy. Unschooled
and insular Quaker girl.
I taxonomized the nation's flora.
How could I name her *Fellow*?
I didn't wait till everyone was gone
to erase it and write in
Honorary Member. It was justice.
Nature hadn't made her one of us.
Then came her King of Denmark's medal.
She had to be called equal,
                even lacking parts.

A DIARY OF MECHANICAL DIFFICULTIES: HAIR

1 JANUARY 1855

Last night I hardly slept, having realized that
today I must put some wires into my transit.
I have risen at dawn to begin. First I remove
the collimating screws, then draw out the tube
and find a brass plate screwed on the diaphragm
which contains the lines. At first I am puzzled—
which screws hold the diaphragm in place? I take
time to study it and see I need turn only two.
Out comes the plate with its three wires
where five should be. I take hairs from my own head,
picking white ones because I have no black to spare.
I put in two by sticking them with sealing wax
dissolved in alcohol. I adjust them firmly
in the grooves, when I see wax on one of the hairs.
That will make it coarser, and it is already
coarse enough. I clean my camel's hair brush
and begin to wash the hair with clear alcohol.
But I wash a wire out—then another, and another.
Now I must put in five perpendicular ones besides
the horizontal which, like the others
has frizzled up and melted away. After an hour
I have them all in, when a rude motion raises them
and I must begin over. It is one o'clock when
I get them in again. I try to replace the diaphragm.
The sealing wax is not dry, and I send the wires agog.
This time they do not jump from the grooves, so I hasten
to remove the brass plate and set them parallel.
I give up for the day.

This is nice ladylike work: to manage such slight threads
and turn such delicate screws. But I shall seek
something finer than my hairs. They look parallel now
but magnified, a very little crook will seem
a billowy wave, and a faint star will hide
in one of the abysses.

18

15 JANUARY 1855

Not only are the hairs too coarse, but they are variable
and curl themselves up at a change of weather.
I wrote to George Bond at Harvard to ask how to get
spider lines. He replies that the web from cocoons
should be used and that I will have difficulty finding
them this time of year. I remember at once having seen
in the Atheneum two I carefully left undisturbed.
I take a ladder and climb to their corner lodging,
armed with a shoebox. At home I find them perfect
and unroll them. But fearing I may not be able
to manage them, I take some hair from Charles' head.
He is under a year old and his hair is remarkably fine.
I make the perpendiculars from spider's webs
breaking them time after time until finally
I get them all in, cross the five with a horizontal
from Charles' head, and wait 24 hours. Exposure to weather
does not change spiderwebs: plainly used to chill,
made to endure it. But Charles' hair has never felt
cold greater than that of the nursery, nor change
more decided than from his mother's arms to his father's.
Charles' hair knots up into a decided curl.

N.B. He may expect ringlets.

DREAM

I am delivered to Harvard
in a black carriage with curtains

The lecture hall churns
men lining the walls, leaning
over balconies

I approach the podium

They continue their conversations

I open my mouth to begin
and my teeth spill out
powdery as chalk

A man in the front row
rushes onstage to gather them

I ask are there questions

and he writes with my tooth
on the blackboard

How do you eat enough to stay alive?

TRAVELLING SOUTH, 1857

1. ON A SAND BAR IN THE MISSISSIPPI

Four days snagged here like flotsam!

after beginning so smoothly,
mythical heroes gliding on gold.
Not like our Atlantic
rearing and bucking.

Oh to stride down Main Street now,
the wind lifting my bonnet . . .
here, walking threatens
to tip our home.

We make the best of confinement:
read Shakespeare, eat oranges
carried from shore.

At first I hoped the tide might deliver
us from this behemoth's back.
But Captain tells me there is none
felt at this place.

Small boats pass, their sailors'
laughter reaches our wheel-house.

Just when I am sure
the 'Magnolia' must petrify here
and we along with her
a rowboat is sent to transfer
Prudence and me to the 'Woodruff'.
We clutch hands as our teacup
whirls in the steamer's great churn.

At last! next stop Cairo
on the river set with snares.

2. IN NEW ORLEANS

Even at dawn the air hangs
in this city of orange turbans,
bouquets of French.

This could be a schoolroom:
men, women, children in rows on long
parallel benches.
Thank the Lord no buyers yet,
no painful examinations.

All stand as we enter
for us to walk between.
The trader tells us speak if we like.
Some do not wait on us
but advertise themselves.
A woman pulls at my shawl
and asks me to buy her.
I am not a housekeeper, I say.
Not married?—her eyes wide with pity.

There is one girl whiter than I.
I cannot answer her
whose past and future speak
so plainly in her face.
What right have I to be homesick?

3. OUTSIDE SAVANNAH

On the path edged with mockingbird calls
we pass through an arch of live-oaks
throwing their arms against heaven.
Low, by our wheels, azalea and jessamine.
Overhead, old man's beard.

Mr. Potter walks us through his neat fields
to their huts. "Call the children

and give us some singing,"
he orders the boy who runs
shouting "Come and sing for massa."

Like bolls they come tumbling
through fields, airborne over fences
until eighteen settle at our feet.
"Early in the morning," sings the lead.
"Let us think of Jesus," offer up the rest.

4. CONCERNING SOUTHERN MEN

Easier to travel alone than in the North.
Gentlemen are courteous and careful
though the finest says *Nigger, bring my horse*
and a fussiness about them makes me feel
they are the woman and I am the man.
Even riverboat captains.

5. IN KENTUCKY

But the propriety—Mammoth Cave
without a gentleman escort?
If two ladies travel alone
they must have the courage of men.

We engage Mat as our guide.
He leads, I am next, Prudence last.
Toward the mouth, land
falls two hundred feet.
We cross a thread of stream,
slip through a buttonhole

into a cloth of night so plush
that our Bengal lamps
hardly find our toes.
Where are the limits,
where are we led?

An hour before I can see
the elliptical chambers, ceilings
like the sky over Vestal Street
in cloudy moonlight.

We clamber over heaps of rock,
descend ladders, wind through
tunnels so low we crouch
their whole length and still
brush the damp tops, the webs.
Then we undo our way,
climb to lofty halls,
cross bridges over nothing.
I must reason myself onward,
glad when we rest on flat rock.
Would I suffer this to get free?

Prudence cocoons herself in a shawl
and swings her lamp on a stick,
a witch from *Macbeth*.
Mat sits lower, dirty tin cup
across his chest a talisman.

Now he descends behind us
with the lights
a dark cloud passes over
the starlit vault and we cry out
to him to come back, we do not
wish to "see" total darkness . . .

When I was four, the Friends kept
Arthur Cooper of Virginia and his family
in the peat diggers' caves
until the marshals sailed back to Boston.

I always wanted wings. I would say not a word
to anyone, just give a few shakes,
a little flap, and begin to rise.

FROM THE LETTERS THAT
SISTER PHEBE BURNED

Dearest Maria,

I swear no thing would make me happier than
for you to look with favor upon the course
which I propose. What could we not do:
your eyes and mine become one pair
uplifted to chart the order of space and sky?

I know you well enough to know that duty
informs your every choice. Believe that I
desire equally to support your parents' needs.
I cannot think, my dear, that they would ask
your care at such great burden to yourself.
What obstacle then to blest conjunction?

I await impatiently your answer and
that day the world must call you *Mrs. Bond*.

THE SINGLE LIFE:
MARIA'S GHOST CONFIDES

What man would have been so foolish as to
fall in love with me? *No*

that is not what I wished to say. See my face.
One guest thought I was the Portuguese

maid at my sister Ann's wedding. They had told him
Maria was the darkest person in the room.

My sisters all married. *In family portraits they
were not prettier than I.*

As a child, my brother Andrew slipped off at dawn
to go whaling. I kneeled hidden

behind crates on the wharf, dressed
in his breeches and cap, to taste

such single life as brothers could find
while sisters stayed on land.

Girls were not allowed on the dock. I smelled tar,
fish, the whale oil. The sailors wore

rings in their ears. From the sailmakers' lofts
songs fell. As I listened, Andrew left.

This is closer. More on this. I used to say
my looks kept from me

the love of a husband but *no again*
it was something unseen

something I wanted that he would get between
and I be unable, unalone

in my watches, half astronomer at his side,
expected wholly in his bed.

Yes. George Bond
and I loved.

I kept his letters hidden, locked in mind
the hour he held my hand.

Now my singleness cannot be married away
I let you praise my

"fine," "dark," "penetrating," impenetrable eyes.

II

"And here I pause to say that I do not like *needles*. With the exception of the magnetic needle, I believe they are too much in use, & I like the worsted needle least of all. In the Bodleian Library is a cabinet labelled 'works of learned ladies,' & on examining the collection, you will find it is made up of samplers, very neatly done, without a doubt, but still *samplers*."

DIARY ENTRY, 1857

CROSSING THE ATLANTIC, THIS REQUEST

Oh please Miss. If you could tell me fartune.

But sure you're an astronomer? Well

what, pray, *can* you tell if not fartunes?

Well why should anyone want to know *that*—

the sun and moon's hour to rise and set.

I was thinkin you'd know how I'd win Gavin

and which pasture we'd be buyin

and who i twas took Michael's cart.

Ohhh, I see then. Is tha *tall*?

MEETING HAWTHORNE

A gray morning at the Derby Museum
made me crave the accents of home.
I was delighted to receive Consul
Hawthorne at my lodgings in Liverpool.
He was both chatty and diffident,
stayed no more than five minutes
during which he took his stovepipe hat
from the table and put it back
once a minute, brushing off specks
I could not see. He looks odd,
not of this earth—as he would.
His hair disperses so much
I wanted to quell it with combs
and brushes and toilet ceremonies.

EN ROUTE TO ROME WITH THE HAWTHORNES

She objected. He promised I'd be no care.
Two days ago this coach was held up.
I have hid my fortune in my stocking;
only a Nor'easter could search me.

After ten hours, twilight is our shroud.
Among the cypresses we see men with guns.
Each drubbing by the road makes our supper
of dry sour bread and goat cheese revolt.

I wish I could sleep, like young Julian
rolled in his corner. He wakes just to
wish the whole dome of St. Peter's were
one mutton chop, and he could eat it up.

Hush, hush. Mrs. Hawthorne grows pale
propped between Una and Rosa. For her husband
our ride must be almost worse than a party.
All roads lead to Rome except this.

MARIA'S GHOST ADDRESSES HAWTHORNE
CONCERNING CHAPTER FIVE OF *THE MARBLE FAUN*, IN WHICH SHE APPEARS

"A needle is familiar to the fingers of them all. A queen, no doubt, plies it on occasion; the woman-poet can use it as adroitly as her pen; the woman's eye, that has discovered a new star, turns from its glory to send the polished little instrument gleaming along the hem of her kerchief, or to darn a casual fray in her dress. The slender thread of silk or cotton keeps them united with the small, familiar, gentle interests of life, the continually operating influences of which do so much for the health of the character, and carry off what would otherwise be a dangerous accumulation of morbid sensibility. . . . Methinks it is a token of healthy and gentle characteristics, when women of high thoughts and accomplishments love to sew; especially as they are never more at home with their own hearts than when so occupied."

Bosh, Mr. Hawthorne. The seam splits
and needs repair.
Yet I was honored to be present.
Amused, because I hate to sew.

But our "dangerous accumulation of morbid sensibility"?
Why did you sit before the fire,
volume of Thackeray open
in your lap, not reading it but
thereby keeping us from you?
In Rome your daughter Una
turned 16. We drank her health
(cold water) and you pronounced this
birthday wish: "May you live happily

and be ready to go when you must."
Why were you so inactive?
Always disappointed?—even
St. Peter's not grand enough.

Did you say "never more at home"
with our own hearts?
Better to ponder the spectroscope
than the pattern of a dress.
To crack geodes than match worsteds.
When I see a woman sew, I think of science.
When she puts an exquisite
fine needle exactly the same distance
from the last stitch as that
stands from the one before, I think
what capacity she has
for using a micrometer, graduating circles.
How she would be at home in stars.

You're right, it's academic
what with sewing machines,
machines to stitch the farthest sky
and even fabricate a novel.
But your attitude prevails
like mold that eats the Roman statues.
Please remember me to Mrs. Hawthorne.
I hope that her neuralgia's passed.

IN ROME

To find rooms
enter
a narrow dark
passage and look
in vain for a door.
Climb
a flight
of stairs.
Find a door
with a string,
and pull.
A woman's mouth appears
at a square
covered with tin,
holes poked therein.
Asks what you
want. You tell.
She says climb
more. You do
and at last reach home,
fifth floor.
The higher the better.
Oh benison
of sun.

I could make a better cart
than those I see on the streets
and I could almost
make better horses than those
that pull the carts.

Holy Week I spend seven hours a day
at St. Peter's. The ladies are seated.
As the rituals unfold
in different parts of the huge building,

black veils streaming the women race
back and forth like furies let loose.

Even statues in the Vatican do not seem *dead*.

Here he was tried
in the Hall of Sopre Minerva
trembling before that tribunal
whose frown was torture,
declaring false his truth.

And the Holy Church likewise
trembling before Galileo who found
in the Book of Nature something
absent from their Book of God.

Two truths cannot conflict . . .

I am at Quaker Sunday Meeting.
It is 1843.

I cannot hear my footsteps for the sand
sprinkled to deaden sound.
On one side I am watched by black hats
on the other, gray bonnets.
Father and Mother sit before the assembly.
I slip in between Ann and Phebe.
No noise jars the peace
but my heart, my shallow breathing.

Though it is August, I shiver.
Why do they ban music and color?
God put color in stars, music in birdsong—
beauty all around like Saturn's ring.
Uncle Henry Pratt, jailed
in England for his faith, wrote it in blood
drawn from his arm. Thoughtless "Discipline"
is my cell. I choose to be disowned . . .

Galileo's greatest heresy to know
earth moves. For this
robed in black and on his knees
to the cardinals he was made to swear never
again would he teach devils' words.

Rising, he whispered what he must to live:
E pur si muove, It does move.

AT THE VATICAN OBSERVATORY

How should I know my heathen feet must not
enter the sanctuary, my woman's robes
not brush the seats of learning. The Father's
eyebrows fly. I feel improper. Later

permission granted. Again I err, supposing
the door which opens to one woman opens
to all. I ask to take with me my Italian
maid who on our evening walks has learned
the names of stars and said them back in her
sweet tongue. Request refused, and swiftly.

The Father's telescope clockwork measures
earth's motion on its axis—persistent
though the Holy Church declared it wrong.
Two centuries: Galileo watches.

I wish to stay after dark to look
at nebulae. Foiled again. The Ave Maria
will ring half-hour in advance of sunset
and I must leave before, like Cinderella
arriving home just as the bell rings out
their warning stay. What do they think I will
become at nightfall? Or what will they?

NEWS FROM FLORENCE: THE CHOLERA

Believers kneel to the Madonna, make processions.
Always after such shows of faith
the number of cases is seen to increase

and the Misericordia, in their masks and gloves
an army of spectres, glide through the streets
night and day, carrying the sick to hospitals.

Those who stay attempt normal life . . .

Mrs. Somerville tells how, driving home late
from a neighbor's villa, her carriage ran against
a cart en route to the burying-ground at Trespiano

and the jolt loosed one of that unbending cargo,
flung him under the wheels
where he snapped like dry limbs in a storm.

Rome sleeps lightly, with death in its ears.

HARRIET HOSMER OF WATERTOWN, MASSACHUSETTS

Rome, sculptor Paul Akers' studio

In strides the pretty girl,
her hands thrust in her pockets,
and begins to rattle
an invitation to ride horseback
over the Campagna which he interrupts
Oh, not with you—I'm afraid to.

So this is Harriet Hosmer.
She is not like other Quakers.
At first troubled by her ways
I later see that she parades
her weaknesses with the conscious power
of one who knows her strength.

She possesses psychic gifts.
When objects vanish, she tells the owner
where they hide. One day out riding
she saw a fence post raise itself
above the ground. In these matters
I try to keep my mind ajar.

Pity her three male friends in Iowa
who boasted men are better climbers.
That summer day she beat them to the top
of what they named Mt. Hosmer.

I do not wonder that she plans
to carve the ancient Queen Zenobia,
once mistress of the Roman East.
Even vanquished, on display in Rome
Zenobia would not bow her regal shoulders,
in captive dignity strode on.

How Miss Hosmer studies to make the woman
express her people's fate.
She learns the gaze from ancient coins.
If she hears that in a church

two hundred miles away she will find
the robes of Eastern Queens
she mounts her horse and rides to see.

In all America no school
would teach Miss Hosmer sculpture.
I think she rules in exile too.

A VISIT TO THE PARIS MORGUE

This is the other side
of the Place de la Concorde at sunrise
this is the assassins' museum
the Académie where Rodin
could study for his Gates of Hell

I am told the regulars arrive each day
detour from their sunlit lives down this alley
to the door that is never locked—
men and women of every age and social rank.

Now schoolboys hang at the glass, point down
at naked women on slabs, anatomy lessons
that turn them laughing to each other
chattering too fast for my comprehension.

The old woman hunched beside me knows
I am foreign and shouts in my ear Vous voyez?
Que pensez-vous de cette pièce?
I do not answer but think

Voyez. Voyeuse
at the window of strangers' most private act.
Shall I call my visit scientific inquiry?
Myself will not be soothed

> *Always the water drips, drips on breaking flesh*
> *and trickles down the stone walls*
> *as if this house sheds tears*
> *this is the crater named Mortal*
> *this makes us make a world without end*

DREAM

I am laboring through the dunes
    air collapses
        the world's becalmed

dune grass points
    green fingers up
        I run and trip

        lie squirming

sand sifts inside my collar
    migrates down my back
        each grain a pin

        the fingers tie me fast

the horseshoe crab
    on whiskered legs advances
        drags its icepick tail

I would scream but have no
    voice to tame
        this ancient bone

MOTHER FALLS ILL

She knows me in the morning
when I bring her tea
but as the sun begins to sink
her language flickers
until my name goes out

Mother who before we all were born
read through two libraries
who hailed words like a shipwrecked soul
how can we sweep your room enough
to keep the dust from filtering in

you move from me beyond the stars
I have no telescope with power
to reach your mind
no observation
to comprehend the chaos

this I fear above all things

not to work
to be lost in darkness on the moor
not knowing which way land or sea
the heavens obscured
and fog the product of my hands

to be locked in endless winter
unable to learn poetry
to receive no mail or news, send none
my observing chair blown off the roof
and covered by drifts

Dear God, let me turn from this glass

ROUGH PASSAGE

yesterday on the steamer to Nantucket
the ocean climbing towers in this season
I felt unwell and retired to the women's cabin
where I laid me down along the bench
and tried to leave my body, send my mind
in spirals to the Northern Star

when two island women in the corner
took up a conversation, "I suppose
Maria Mitchell did some big things—
people say so—but she is awfully homely!"
"Well, yes" hesitates the other "she is,
but you must admit she has fine eyes."

which I kept shut upon the things
that people say: the pitch, the roll . . .

AN INVITATION

Cheers for Thomas Higginson, who writes "Nature
has everything to dread from constraint, nothing
from liberty." Mr. Lincoln thinks so too.
When he issues the Emancipation Proclamation,
Matthew Vassar signs beside his name.

Can it be the chain of ignoble submissions
will break? Mr. Babcock, trustee of the proposed
Vassar Female College brings an offer:
I teach young women astronomy, lead them
toward that destiny for which they are endowed.

I feel myself urged on by idiotic tirades
in the press. Reverend Todd promises that women,
so delicate, will die if they attempt
to go through college. Dr. Clarke predicts
no less than ruination of the Commonwealth.

Thank God for some sane men! Dr. Wilder
holds all science possible, proper for a woman.
Harriet Hosmer travelled far to find
a doctor who would teach her the human body.
Without it, she could not make her sculpture art.

The trustees seem convinced I am the one
to fill the void. I only wonder am I
equal to this place—no college degree myself,
no passport to such regions. How am I fit?
I believe in women even more than in astronomy.

THE CIVIL WAR SUSPENDS MORE
FRUITFUL ENTERPRISE

Of course the Vassar College project halts.
Women who have never left before leave home
to nurse, roll bandages, give out supplies,
raise money for this war. I pray it ends
before our nation is rent beyond repair.

The South I saw five years ago
showed me a system flawed: where one class
does all the thinking and the other all the work
masters should be active thinkers, and slaves
ready workers. But both were listless and inert.

Still, how can a soldier be a Christian?
My own brother Andrew nearly died
at Vicksburg. What for, slaughter of ourselves?
Do the parties solve by killing what they would not
solve by love? No answers. Only sky.

III

"We put the solar eye-piece on to the telescope, and we protect the eye with a colored glass, and we are ready to scrutinize the sun's surface. Another lesson is soon learned. The heat collected by this great burning glass is intense; it does not fall on the eye, but it must fall somewhere, and where it falls, it burns. Many a delicate handkerchief, and many a thin, gauze-like sleeve scorched & burned beneath our glass before we learned to adopt the hydropathic treatment, & wrap ourselves in wet towels if we wished to make prolonged observations."

FROM "WATCHING THE SUN," 1870

STUDY WITH PROFESSOR MITCHELL

That first year my heart thumped
if we met along the path to the Observatory,
air so charged with her high voltage.
Her "unexpectedness" they call it.
Thought speeds straightway to her lips.

In time I saw her kindness,
learned her forthright way.
She asks nothing of her students
she will not urge upon herself.

She hates to give us grades, part
of what she deems police work.
She never takes attendance, never
asks us what we may read in books.

The highest title she confers
is none at all. *Whitney, Blackwell, King—*
we are lucky if we lose a prefix.
I judge this the equality of Quakers.

She and Dr. Avery our physician
are our two female professors.
One we see during hours;
for us the other is always home.

We visit her in her parlor
with the bust of Mary Somerville,
the painting of Humboldt in his study,
the books, and for the first time
some of us can see what women
by strict scholarship attain.

Julia's father has forbidden her
to take more courses in Astronomy.
Why should we not love
our constant model? Are men hurt
if they admire male professors?

I would not change her looks
for any pretty, regulation type:
the deep-set eyes and shaggy brows,
the large, undaunted mouth.

When Meg our classmate died
Professor Mitchell said how hard
it must have been for her
to leave such a beautiful body.

At Professor Mitchell's Dome Party
each June we come to breakfast
and to celebrate each other in verse.
Outside we pose for photographs.
A crowd of laughing girls
and their stately, gray-haired teacher—
the granite sundial in a rose garden.

STAGEFRIGHT

Congress of the Association for the
Advancement of Women, Syracuse, 1875

We gather in an opera house and I am no performer.
A President too nervous to eat breakfast
I must lead our meeting as my stomach churns.
In ancient Syracuse, Demosthenes
the Athenian general was put to death.
Another tried his lungs against the waves.
Today I would be general and orator too.
Throat, do not rebel.

                The hall seats one thousand
seven hundred and every place is filled.
Scores of women with babies in their arms,
rough men in the aisles, schoolboys and girls
near the platform, books in hand.
My heart pounds so—I wait frozen
at the podium until the clamor dies and then
before I say a word a man at the rear shouts
"Louder!" and everyone is laughing,
myself among them, and quiet must be restored.
I lift the gavel but do not strike it.

Does the hall grow still?
                I cannot believe
so many will listen when I ask them to.

MARIA'S GHOST HAUNTS
PHYLLIS SCHLAFLY

We also wear the chains we forge in life.
Fear not. Your reclamation, then.
These are the shadows of things that have been.

See this Cooking class. The year is 1886,
the students scarcely 12 years old.
Where are the boys? Must boys not cook
unless as famous chefs, paid as well
as President of Harvard College?
Almost 2000 years one half the race
has starved her mind to better feed the body
of the other half

                   and yet you cry confusion
in identity when boys learn Home Economics,
girls take Shop. You praise an 'old-fashioned,
proper lady' who cooks her husband's breakfast
and chastise her whose husband cooks his own.

Anne Sexton lied to keep her time
to write uninterrupted, telling callers
she had to check the oven, test a cake.

These are the shadows of things that are still.

I show you Mary Somerville in 1827
secretly translating Laplace's *Mécanique Céleste*.
The doorbell sounds. She hides her papers
under sofa cushions, lifts the latch
to find a neighbor just stopped by to chat.
She brews tea, they talk of weather
and the new Archbishop, her mind half-straining
toward her papers the neighbor sits upon.

Yet you claim that in the drawing room
a gracious hostess does her highest work.

We also wear the chains of fear.

No confusion where identity is not.
For example, poor Mrs. Whatzis—

> I am Tommy's wife.
> Growing up, I was Dr. Bill's daughter.
> Then became Jen's mother, Sal's mother, Bunny's
> mother, Frank and Ed's mother.
> The Christian woman is most truly liberated, free
> to do what God has called her to.

When God called, how did she know her name?

Hear yourself! you rail against
'a bunch of marital misfits who . . .
replace woman as virtue and mother
with prostitute, swinger, and lesbian.'
Really.

These are the shadows of fears you forge.

Like you, I do go on. But let a ghost take liberties.
As you are now, so once was I;
as I am now, so will be you.

Look farther down this rutted path.
Your kind shall lift, propel you till that law
you so despise shall stand,
the era you call ended shall begin.

Follow me. Across the country
your latest book is absent from the shelves
of libraries, is not available in stores.
See the scales: one grain of right outweighs
a bushel of custom. That grain begins the field
and gives us food, not shadows. *Take heed,*

our parting moment now

MATTHEW VASSAR READS HIS MORNING MAIL; OR, INTEMPERATE TEMPERANCE

Look what came today, this
letter from a graduate
who had a full-tuition scholarship
through all four years and now
conceives it is her duty
to chide the Founder
for the way he made his money,

'A college foundation laid in beer
will never prosper.'

Well it was *good* brew, wasn't it.
And where would she have learned to form
opinions if it hadn't been for beer.

MATTHEW VASSAR'S SOUL LIFTS OFF

A bird at my ear
a flame beneath my ribs
then dark

I see my body
slumped upon the chair
the Trustees
rushing over
rushing in and out

Friends
don't hurry

My resignation letter
sprawls
at page eleven

Where
was I?

Just past urging
Miss Mitchell
must be kept although
Astronomy is small

I was about
to say . . . no matter

You saw
when Mr. Lincoln
rode the black-draped train to Springfield
I climbed
aboard to place magnolia
on his coffin

Cut some
for me—there, the tree
that blooms
along our college
path, its roots are deep
and spreading

FATHER DIES

Four vacant days I have not been to the Dome.
No one can lead me through unearthly night.
Where are you teacher, Father, to teach me time
without you? If I believed you fixed and light
above like stars we shared, then sleep could come
release me for a while, healing might
begin. I see you only under ground
on Prospect Hill with Mother, the iron fence
a border none of us can shout beyond.
One stormy night you lectured to an audience
on storms, said *Even now death flies the wind*.
Next day the sailor washed ashore, eyes wild.
Where are you, Father? I am no one's child.

REMEMBER THE SISTER OF WILLIAM

Caroline Herschel (1750–1848)

No woman has the right to lose her self
in such devotion to her brother's work
that her life ends when he crosses the gulf

twenty years before her. You were more than half
a person, Caroline. What you did spurs
women. Yet you were not right to lose your self:

what you did not will warn us. Serf,
drudge, at 14 scouring pots while he took
endless lessons. Life could not engulf

him. Notice how the world goes deaf
when women tell their equal need to fathom dark.
Though woman has rights, to lose her self

is still the world's idea of charm. Enough.
God bless my father. My mother's love of books.
My own life bends toward that gulf

they and you have leapt. Grief
stops there. Too late! In life let women mark
no woman has the right to lose her self—
to end when any *he* has crossed the gulf.

THE TOTAL ECLIPSE OF THE SUN

Burlington, Iowa   August 7, 1869

We are at the College by 9 a.m.
and soon humanity decorates the fences.
Nothing can convince them
the eclipse will happen outside
telescopes. Finally the authorities
persuade them to climb down.
The instrument maker corrects
some derangements due to travel
and we are ready to wait.

We wait, we scarcely breathe,
the moon is not on time, then all at once

an ink begins to spill upon
the limb of sun and as it spreads
narrowing the golden curve of light
as it breaks to brilliant lines
and points, the total phase draws near

thin clouds have drifted
toward the sun, the Mississippi goes leaden
and a sickly green washes over the land

Venus shines on one side of the sun,
Mercury the other; Arcturus overhead
and Saturn rising in the East

the cattle low, birds cry painfully,
fireflies start up in the leaves
and when the last light quenches
a wave of voices lifts from villages below

the corona bursts forth
encircling the sun, streamers
unroll for millions of miles in space

two prominences glow on the right
of the burning disk, a twentieth
of the moon's diameter, and shaped
like half-blown morning glories
pink and white, with violet intermingling

the moon moves on, billowy forms arising
near its vertex shift within themselves,
a flicker at the moon's center and
another flower rushes out

                    to bloom the sun . . .

No wonder there are sun-worshippers!—

that old hyperbole for man. I claim for us
such light and constancy. My young women
never turned to see the trespasser who moved
among our telescopes, fluttering green veils,
the man in woman's clothes.
They would have kept observing
though the ground beneath them gaped.

THE WORDS OF THE TRESPASSER
CLOSELY VEILED

Yes, but why are they really here?
Some ritual of darkness,
some man-reviling sport?
Unnatural behind cold instruments
they hide their female shape.

Beth will never miss her things this afternoon.
They bar intruders but I walk among them
since it has begun. No time for questions.
They are so fixed at their lenses
a grizzly bear could pass unseen

       oh I am the one with secrets now
       under these skirts, I am inside the circle

even as light begins to seep through dark.
There! the elder's arm presses the young shoulder—
at "dawn" they all embrace.

DREAM

a rat slips through a crack

I gag on rancid light
the mold of cellars

pain railroads down my legs
let help find a vein

this is a hospital for mothers and children
through a telescope I scan my womb

Mother is my doctor
head nurse wears Phebe's face

I climb a ladder toward a view
simple problem but I've lost the trick

and turn to watch my scream spread
brilliant on the sheet

Mother catch my child

nearing she presents me with
the lump of coal

PARTIAL ECLIPSE

This morning I have struggled
hours with three elementary formulae
from Loomis, easiest algebra I ever knew.
Continually I was mistaking figures.
Perhaps my glasses are too weak.

Why is it painful to know
my old assistant has obtained employment?
Why should she not be as willing
to work for me as for a man?

Just now the electric light blinks.
The buzzing in my ears has persisted
though insect season is long past.
I must sometimes halt my lectures
in surrender to the mounting din.

Why does a group of colored people
sing here to raise money?
Why should Vassar have more duty
educating slaves than Harvard?

My new teeth and old shoes trouble me.
No consolation that in youth new shoes
hurt and old teeth kept me awake.
I have written the letters
I owe, have paid all my debts.

Who does a shadow belong to—
is it the property of the person who receives,
is it the sun's property?
Is my shadow mine?

LETTER TO DR. AVERY

June 14, 1888

My dear Doctor,

Vassar calls me Professor
Emeritus and asks me to accept
a free home at the college.
I am pleased to decline.

The letter did me good
after all our work
to make the college
pay us like its men.

I have put my observatory
at the oppoiste* shore
in Kate's backyard
surrounded by apple trees.
I aim not at discoveries
but at health for yours

MM

*Isn't this a peculiar spelling?
Do you remember how I once splled
'flox'?

MARIA MITCHELL IN THE GREAT BEYOND
WITH MARILYN MONROE

What would my life have been with your face?
Once someone said I had good eyes. Mostly
on canvas, in photographs, I half turned away.
The camera, they say, was your most faithful lover.

> No one ever told me I was pretty when I was
> a little girl. All little girls should be told
> they're pretty, even if they aren't.

Little girls should hear the truth.
No one could make a beauty of me. I knew.
And Quaker Discipline decreed: "Be not conformed
to this world, but be ye transformed
by the renewing of your mind."
A child in my closet-size study, I hung a sign—
Maria is busy. Do not knock.

> When I was 8 my foster family made me wash
> every dish for 5 cents a month.

Dear child, how could fame repair such loss,
your mother's mind broken like her parents'
and brother's before. Though a woman, I
faltered when Mother's mind cast off from me.

> The same year, at the boardinghouse the nice
> man showed me a game, and when

I saw! They disbelieved, and you began to stammer.
What man on earth isn't selfish?
My sister died thankful never to have been naked
before her husband. I never married.
Come walk with me. Smell the ocean
and pick daphne, grapes, heart's ease.

Do you know how I got here? Three days before
at a party I wrote in the guest book
under Residence, *Nowhere*.

And now you live everywhere at once
whose ambition was to be men's earthly star.
Here are stars you can trust:
Sirius, Canopus, Arcturus, Vega, Capella,
Betelgeuse, Altair, Aldebaran.
Say these, Norma Jeane.
We are women learning together.

MARIA'S GHOST CONTEMPLATES HER PRESERVERS

The longer I live
the more I value the love
of my own sex, neither vain
nor fawning

Dr. Emilia Belserene—
beautiful brightness it means—
director of the observatory in my name
praise you on the narrow winding stairway to the dome
and at the 5-inch telescope, gift of the "Women of America"
bless you at your Smith-Corona
continuing under blue fluorescent light
and summer evenings waiting for the clouds to part

Dr. Jane Stroup, guardian
of my papers, shielding the glass cases with muslin
so our photographs won't disappear
praise you who let a stranger use the copier
who polishes my Dolland telescope that tracked the comet
praise your keys to lock the cabinet
that holds the notebooks and my journals
sister Phebe saw fit not to burn

Dr. Louise Hussey
keeper of Nantucket's oldest stories
I read on winter days till I was full
may the inner vault maintain its temperature control
the words on parchment fix
praise your steps from desk to stacks
bless your cane, your ancient auto
you at the wheel, and keep you from the latest flu

Dear women my preservers
the world is so broad
I reach at every nerve
to pull the curtain aside

NOTES

THE CHARLESTOWN ENTERPRISE EXCLUSIVE is excerpted from an un-
dated article, MM Science Library, Nantucket, Massachusetts. . . . "MISS
MITCHELL'S COMET" so named by Loomis in *The Recent Progress of Astron-
omy* (NY: Harper's, 1856). The comet is described in notebooks of MM's
father. . . . DR. ASA GRAY EATS CROW: H. Mitchell reports the erasure in
a biographical notice of MM for *Proceedings of the American Academy of Arts
and Sciences*, 1890. . . . A DIARY OF MECHANICAL DIFFICULTIES: HAIR
is mainly quoted from MM's diary, Kendall, pp. 39–41. . . . TRAVELLING
SOUTH uses language from MM's journals, Kendall, Ch. IV. MM was
chaperone to Prudence, daughter of Gen'l. Swift, a Chicago banker. Ending
of poem suggested by a story MM wrote for her niece Fanny Macy. . . .
FROM THE LETTERS: George Bond, son of the Director of Harvard College
Observatory, was said by his daughter to have loved MM, Wright,
p. 68. . . . MEETING HAWTHORNE and EN ROUTE TO ROME transcribe
sections of MM's journals, Kendall, Ch. V. . . . MARIA'S GHOST AD-
DRESSES HAWTHORNE: Stanza 3 contains ideas expressed in MM's "The
Need of Women in Science," *Papers Read at the Fourth Congress of Women*
(Washington, DC: Todd Bros., 1877). . . . IN ROME and AT THE VATICAN
OBSERVATORY transcribe from MM's journals, Kendall, Ch. VI. . . . HAR-
RIET HOSMER is a composite from Kendall and information in *Letters &
Memories*, ed. C. Carr (NY: Moffat, Yard, & Co., 1912). . . . A VISIT TO THE
PARIS MORGUE: In fact Rodin was 18 when MM visited Paris, and would
not begin the Gates of Hell for another 30 years. The details of the Morgue
are suggested by Zola's *Thérèse Raquin*, 1867, Trans., Leonard Tancock (NY:
Penguin, 1962). MM struggled to believe in an afterlife. . . . MOTHER
FALLS ILL: MM feared inheriting the "brain disease" her mother suffered
during her last years. . . . ROUGH PASSAGE: The anecdote appears in
F. Wood, *Earliest Years At Vassar*, a reprint from *Vassar Miscellany*, January,
1909. The theme of MM's homely appearance recurs throughout her jour-
nals. . . . AN INVITATION and THE CIVIL WAR use Wright, Ch. 8. MM: "I
believe in women even more than I do in astronomy." . . . STUDY WITH
PROFESSOR MITCHELL contains impressions recorded by MM's Vassar
students, primarily Mary King Babbitt, *Maria Mitchell As Her Students Knew
Her* (Poughkeepsie, NY: Underhill, 1912); and Harriet Prescott Spofford,
"Maria Mitchell" in *Brief Biographies of Maria Mitchell & Other Papers*, MM
Science Library. The closing image is Alice Stone Blackwell's. . . . STAGE-
FRIGHT: Stanza 2 is mainly quoted from Kendall, pp. 258–9. . . . MARIA'S
GHOST HAUNTS: MM reacts to a visit to The Cobbitt School, Lynn, Mas-
sachusetts, 1886. Stanzas 10 and 12 quote Schlafly, *The Power of the Positive
Woman* (New Rochelle, NY: Arlington House, 1977). MM: "One grain of
right outweighs a bushel of courtesy." . . . MATTHEW VASSAR READS is
told in Wood. . . . REMEMBER THE SISTER OF WILLIAM contains views
expressed in MM's "Remembrance of the Herschels," *The Century Illustrated
Monthly Magazine*, October, 1889, in *Brief Biographies*. . . . THE TOTAL
ECLIPSE: The descriptive language is essentially MM's, from "The Total
Eclipse of 1869," *Hours At Home*, October, 1869 in *Brief Biographies*. Though a
heavily veiled stranger did appear, the man in woman's clothes is mine. . . .
PARTIAL ECLIPSE: MM's late journals (1882–9) evince her waning powers.
Last stanza uses Wright, p. 238. . . . LETTER TO DR. AVERY is mainly
quoted from Item 34, MM Science Library. . . . MARIA MITCHELL IN THE
GREAT BEYOND: MM to the class of 1876 at Vassar: "We are women study-
ing together."

ACKNOWLEDGMENTS

Some of these poems have appeared with slightly different titles in the following publications:

American Poetry Review: "Maria Observes Halley's Comet, 1835," "Maria's Ghost Considers Interpretation by Freud," "Maria's Ghost Haunts Phyllis Schlafly"

Clockwatch Review: "Maria's Ghost Considers the Reappearance of Halley's Comet in 1985," "Maria's Mother Falls Ill," "Rough Passage"

Prairie Schooner: "An Invitation," "At the Vatican Observatory," "En Route to Rome with the Hawthornes," "In Rome," "Maria Meets Hawthorne," "Maria Mitchell in the Great Beyond with Marilyn Monroe," "Maria's Father Dies," "Maria's Ghost Addresses Hawthorne Concerning Chapter Five of *The Marble Faun*, in Which She Appears," " 'Miss Mitchell's Comet,' " "*The Charleston Enterprise* Exclusive on Maria," "The Single Life: Maria's Ghost Confides"

The Radical Teacher: "Study with Professor Mitchell," "The Total Eclipse of the Sun"

The Worcester Review: "Concerning Maria's Admission to the American Academy of Arts and Sciences, Dr. Asa Gray Eats Crow," "Maria Dreams," "Maria Travels South"

Vassar Quarterly: "Study with Professor Mitchell"

POETRY FROM ALICE JAMES BOOKS